Coming to Terms with Power

with Power

Briony Martin
Journalist and
Ordinand in Diocese of London

GW00706130

GROVE BOOKS LIMITED
RIDLEY HALL RD CAMBRIDGE CB3 9HU

Contents

The Cover Illustration is by the author

Copyright © Briony Martin 1999

First Impression August 1999
ISSN 0262-799X
ISBN 1 85174 410 X

1
Introduction

On Friday last week Olara Otunnu flew into London. Otunnu is the UN Secretary General's Special Representative for Children in Armed Conflict. He had recently left the Albanian village of Kukes and what he saw there had shocked him 'to the core.'

'In a fortnight—no, mostly during one week,' he said, 'over 300,000 people had arrived in this tiny border settlement: they flooded the little town. The sheer volume and speed of the exodus took everyone by surprise, yet so little has been done to help them since they arrived.' He saw people living in garages, warehouses or just on open ground, in tractors and trailers, with inadequate food and little water or shelter. 'And these are simple country people,' he said, 'with no international influence or contacts to help them.'

But he has. He talks to everyone. He flew to Tirana to see the President of Albania; he flew to Geneva for a press conference; he flew to Macedonia and spoke to General Jackson. Then he set off for Rome, intending to discuss it with the Vatican Secretary of State.

He is very concerned that, as a war ends, the needs of women and children should be central, not an afterthought. To this end he works tirelessly to persuade leaders to raise this issue at the peace table. In Burundi, the Sudan and Colombia, he seems to be winning.

And is he optimistic? He pauses. 'I am a person of faith and of hope—the hope that springs from faith. When the bad side of people takes over, evil can triumph. But the opposite can happen.' And he is ready with examples. He spoke of a doctor working tirelessly for years in a battered, understaffed Sudanese hospital; he spoke again of those Albanians, the poorest people in Europe, actively welcoming refugees into their homes while the wealthy West dithers. And he told me about Maggie and Beatriz [who] tell each other their stories and agree to work together, Hutu and Tutsi, with orphans.

[He believes] that, when you cut through the infrastructure of warfare, you find local people who can be extraordinary. 'Here is the policy you should adopt—go women; go children; go local. That is how these societies will be redeemed.'

From 'Mr Fixit's mission' by Sue Gaisford, *The Tablet*, 1 May 1999

Christians are very coy about the word 'power.' To link power and Christianity in the light of Jesus' teaching about 'turning the other cheek' and his status as one who 'made himself nothing,' can seem inappropriate or unspiritual.

Yet power is a reality and, though it can be used for immense evil, it can be the key to doing immense good. Less familiar and less popular parts of the gospels tell us that Jesus came 'not to bring peace but a sword' (Mt 10.34). Christ's mission was not simply to persuade individuals to love their neighbours. It was to radically challenge a system in which those with power abused those without it.

To offer this challenge Jesus had to get involved with the messy realities of human life, showing us a different way to use our power—and our powerlessness. As followers of Christ who long to change the world with him, we must do likewise. It is too easy to bypass engagement and settle for a comfortable, powerless faith. Instead we must find a way to channel our rage against injustice and evil into a genuine alternative to offer the world.

This booklet aims to help us begin to do just that. It explores the power dynamics at work in human and divine life and goes on to suggest creative ways of relating to the power and powerlessness we experience in ourselves, in the society we live in and in the God we worship.

Inner work is required to stimulate our thinking and feeling about power and so each chapter opens or closes with a 'to do or not to do' exercise designed to kick start our explorations.[1] Most 'to do or not to do's' are suitable for use by both individuals and groups—perhaps in a prayer time, a house group, a staff meeting or just among friends and family.

To Do or Not To Do: A Meditation on Power

Take five minutes to consider the word power. Have a pen and paper handy if you like.

Power.
- What thoughts does it spark off? What feelings does it evoke? Are there questions or opinions or memories that go with it? Does it make you feel positive or negative—hopeful or afraid?
- Think of a time when you felt powerful. How did it make you feel? What was good about it and what was not so good?
- Think of a time when you felt powerless. How did this make you feel? Again—what was good about it and what was not so good about it?
- Turn your attention away from human power and powerlessness and think of a moment or situation when God seemed powerful. How did God's power make you feel? And what was good and not so good about that?
- And again, think of a time when God seemed powerless. How did this powerlessness affect you? What was good and what was bad?

---

1 The phrase 'to do or not to do' comes from Gabrielle Roth, *Sweat Your Prayers* (Dublin: Newleaf, 1997).

2
Power — A Fact of Life

The word power causes different reactions in different people. For some it will spark off hope, for some suspicion, for some temptation. Some will think of power in society—the police, the monarchy, the justice system or a boss at work. Some will think of the power of God, perhaps wondering at creation or questioning a time when God's power was absent. For some it will bring up a sense of powerlessness or a bad experience of power exercised by someone else, perhaps an abusive relationship or a rejected application. For some it will have positive connotations—the taking of power by the black majority in South Africa, the gaining of new responsibilities at work which finally gave the chance to 'get things done.'

Power is an extremely complex subject but one thing is certain: we cannot ignore its presence in our lives. And it is because different manifestations of power and powerlessness are so much a part of our day to day experience that the subject is so complicated.

Power is about action. 'Ability to do or to act; vigour, energy; active property,' says *The Concise Oxford Dictionary*. Power is the ability to *do* something to someone or something else—the ability to effect change. By contrast, we are powerless when we have no ability to control, influence or act on things and instead find things done to us or happening to us.

Sometimes we are more powerful than others. As a parent, as a manager or group leader, as a member of wealthy Western society, we have a say about what happens to us, an ability to choose things and the opportunity to make things happen to other people.

Sometimes we are less powerful than others. As an unemployed person, as the rejected one in a relationship breakdown, as a member of the losing party in an election, we lack the ability to control our own destiny.

And we also find this fact of power differences in our relations with God. As our creator, sustainer and life-giver, God is always more powerful than us. And yet sometimes God seems powerless in the face of natural disasters or the human capacity for evil.

Whether we identify with the powerful or the powerless, it is a fact of life that some people and nations are stronger, wealthier, luckier, more powerful than others. And these power differences are very often expressed in violence and injustice. The powerful become aggressors, the powerless become victims and power itself becomes a means of oppression.

In fact, power is neutral. An ability to 'do' can be essential if good is to be achieved—for example pushing someone away from danger or speaking persuasively against injustice. But if the link between being having the power to dominate and an actual dominating action is not qualified by concern for the weak, power simply becomes a means to harm, steal or shout down.

Power in the hands of human beings is at once a creative opportunity and a dangerous temptation. Yet it is one of the fundamental building blocks of the universe and part of the fundamental structure of the way things are. God is the *source* of power and the power we experience as a fact of our lives finds its beginning in the assertive, outward action of God that created the universe in the first place. Power—the ability to do things—began life, and is the dynamic force by which life is sustained. Therefore, though it can be corrupted and abused, power is fundamental to protecting life and, argue theologians like Paul Tillich, crucial to bringing about and maintaining love and justice: 'One could say that constructive social ethics are impossible so long as power is looked at with distrust.'[2]

Our theology often lets us down here, presenting us with a choice between a weak but loving God and a powerful but careless one. But if power comes from God and is a part of the creation which God saw and called good, then our understanding of power and of God is stretched. And it is in this stretching that we are freed to tackle ourselves as we really are and the world as it really is—places where power can be destructive, alienating and oppressive but where it can also be strong, safe and good.

To Do or Not To Do: A Discussion
Consider the following passages:

1. The preacher was in the pulpit, raised so high above the rapt congregation that those in the front row had to crane their necks to see her. She was speaking clearly and loudly, occasionally referring to her notes and with a slight tremor in her voice that told them she believed in what she said. And what she said was dynamite. They had heard about her of course, the new preaching sensation from the North. 'She'll have you out of your seats' the rumours promised; and it was true. Her words made sense, making the challenges look achievable and God seem close enough to reach out and touch.

2. On the day of the FA cup final the tube train was full of police officers. Alongside the expectant fans in their conflicting red and black, the presence of the officers made us feel a strange mixture of comfort and fear. It is not often you get close enough to an on-duty policeman to study the handcuffs, truncheon and CS spray canisters dripping off their belts. And on this busy Saturday the crush took us just a little bit too close for com-

2   Paul Tillich, Love, Power and Justice (London: Oxford University Press, 1954) p 12.

fort. But the strange thing about being so close was that you could also see their faces, and they all looked so kind—just like your Dad or your big brother really. When they got off with the fans at Wembley we did not know whether to be glad or sorry.

3. I remember visiting maternal grandparents in Devon as a child. On Saturday mornings the first thing to penetrate the night-time nest of quilts and blankets was my grandmother whistling over the radio news bulletin. And then, as sleep gave way to reluctant wakefulness the sound grew and the sensations pushed at the door until they were in and tumbling over each other in a rush of shipping forecast, frying bacon, steaming tea, burning toast and low laughter, and, as if smells and sounds were messengers, we found ourselves—cousins, brothers, parents, aunties—drawn to the table, a family in eggs and bacon.

Identify the different sorts of power in action in the three passages. Consider how each one could be used for good, or misused and abused.

3

Power and Human Society

So how do human beings relate to power? How do we deal with this fact of life that is so essential for good to be protected yet so vulnerable to misuse?

Humanity has always struggled with power and powerlessness and we find a microcosm of this struggle in the Old Testament stories that undergird our Christian faith—stories with resonances well beyond the confines of ancient Israel.

Like any other human society, the Israelites are grappling with how to organize themselves. At the Exodus, Israel has been dramatically rescued from slavery and made a nation in its own right by the life-giving power of God. But Israel's independence is qualified by the continuing presence of the overarching divine rescuer. He gives commandments designed to curb potential excesses of human power and to protect people from each other: 'You shall have no other gods before me. You shall not make for yourself an idol, You shall not misuse the name of the LORD your God. Remember the Sabbath day. You shall not murder. You shall not commit adultery. You shall not steal. You shall not give false testimony. You shall not covet your neighbour's house' (Ex 20).

At first the new community expressed their dependence on God by relying on the fluid and charismatic leadership of a series of 'judges' who arose as circumstances demanded. But building a functioning society proved increasingly difficult in the multi-cultural, war-bound context of the promised land and Israel was soon demanding that the nation's leadership and authority structure be guaranteed in the form of a monarch (1 Sam 8.5).

In the historical books like Samuel and Judges we read about the institutionalized power of Israel's kings that results. First Saul, then David and his descendants, hold power in the community and are able to control and direct its affairs. But although God works with the new system, the kings (and the whole community with them) are quickly corrupted.

In Isaiah 58 the people are condemned by Isaiah the prophet for exploiting their workers, quarrelling and fighting among themselves and oppressing the weak. They are urged instead to loose the chains of injustice and set the oppressed free. Neglect of the weak is a key concern for the prophets, as is the failure to recognize that power is not a personal right, but a gift from God to be stewarded. They take the side of those on the margins of society, calling for an end to the self-protecting human power of the kings and a return to dependence on God in radical relinquishment and humility. Amos condemns the women of Bashan who 'oppress the poor and crush the needy'

(4.1). 'Hate evil and love good and establish justice in the gate,' he continues. 'It may be that the LORD, the God of hosts, will be gracious to the remnant of Joseph' (5.15).

Both kings and prophets wield power, one holding onto it to guarantee the functioning of society, the other calling for it to be let go in a continual questioning of humanity's ability to guarantee anything. And the life of Israel swings like a pendulum between the two extremes. When the power of kings compromises the weak, the prophets step in to redress the balance. But as the prophetic challenge is heard, accepted and institutionalized it must itself become open to further challenge from the margins.

As this archetypal human drama is played out on the small stage of Israel's history it emerges that neither the kings nor the prophets have in themselves the complete answer to the question of how to deal with power. Kings and institutions are so obviously corrupted and corruptible, yet they spring from the inevitable and natural human desire for structure and certainty. Prophets, though they speak up for the oppressed and envision liberating new futures for all, nevertheless do not pretend to be practically capable of running the country.

Prophetic Critique of Power

However, the continual prophetic critique of the kings is more than just a negative reaction to human failings. It is a positive reminder that there is another way of doing things—a way of wielding power so that all benefit, a way of organizing society so that the weak are nurtured and empowered. And this messianic future is not just an idealistic prediction. It is a challenge to be lived out now by the prophets' listeners. In Psalm 72, the ideal king is one who will 'deliver the needy who cry out, the afflicted who have no-one to help, [who] will rescue them from oppression and violence' (12, 14). Kings and people are meant to be building a world where 'the wolf will live with the lamb, the leopard will lie down with the goat, the calf and the lion and the yearling together; and a little child will lead them' (Is 11.6). This vision of the future, in which power differences between weak and strong do not prevent them living together in equality and peace, foreshadows the teachings of Jesus. And it emerges later in Revelation. At the end of time, symbols of earthly hierarchy and dominance are broken down within the ultimate glory of God: 'I did not see a temple in the city, because the Lord God Almighty and the Lamb are its temple. The nations will walk by its light, and the kings of the earth will bring their splendour into it' (21.22, 24).

The Old Testament story about human beings gaining power, only to be challenged to use it differently, is told over and again in contemporary church and society. For example, new Labour's vision of the third way for British politics stood as a prophetic challenge to the excesses of Thatcherism; now the prophets find themselves in government being accused of excessive control. Likewise, the ordination of women to the ministerial priesthood sprang from a prophetic challenge to the institution from the powerless margins; now that women find themselves part of the power structure, they must not forget that they have 'pursued power in order to redistribute it, to circulate it more widely, specifically to those who have formerly held lesser shares.'[3]

Contemporary Attitudes

Unlike Old Testament Israel, contemporary society is not calling for a king. Our culture has already heard and responded to prophetic voices from the democratic movement, feminism and the green lobby, leading us to reject power structures like church, family and state that are seen to have been used to abuse and oppress. We no longer see ourselves as the subjects of those in positions of power. Instead we are free individuals with a vote, who expect to have a say in the running of our lives.

There is a deep ambivalence in society towards any power or authority structures that tell us what to do or how to think. We increasingly question, distrust and disrespect those who hold positions of power and have re-understood them not as figures of control but as service providers who are there to meet our needs—the police force has become the police service, the patient the client and the leader the facilitator.

The Israelite prophets envisaged a return to dependence on the prior power of God when they preached against corruption. But for us, the rejection of potentially abusive power structures leads not to renewed dependence on a power beyond us but to a new emphasis on the power of the individual. Although the prophets rejected those who abused their power, nonetheless they still believed in the divine power source—God, the life giver. Contemporary society sees such an explanation as part of the very structure it is trying to escape.

Theologians like Daphne Hampson interpret Christianity as a system in which the individual is ruled by an authoritative divine Father. She criticizes it not only on the grounds of sexism but because it denies the autonomy of self that is the foundation for equality.[4] Lacking faith in the authoritative God it has been taught to believe in, contemporary society has lost faith in any big story—the idea of a universal meaning just is not valid anymore.

Ironically, whatever the gains of individualism in terms of minority rights and free speech, an individualistic society does not protect the weak any more than a structured and hierarchical one. With privatisation as the alter-

---

3 Margaret Miles, quoted in Catherine Prelinger, Episcopal Women (New York: Oxford University Press Inc, 1992) pp 339–40.
4 See Daphne Hampson (ed), Swallowing a Fishbone (Great Britain: SPCK, 1996).

native to the oppressive nanny state, people must protect themselves, and some are more able to do this than others. In his book *The Powers That Be,* Walter Wink argues that despite rejecting spiritual absolutes, very powerful and very real spiritual values (or spiritualities) underlie nations and organizations as well as individuals.[5] And these values are more often than not based on a structure of dominance in which the strong oppress the weak. Once again the age old power dynamics based on differences in strength are in action, but with no absolutes, no qualification of strength, nothing concrete by which abuses can be checked.

Yet contemporary society also evidences an alternative to the bankrupt power vacuum that exists in the gap between a hierarchical society and an individualistic one. And in this it points to a different sort of God. Consider the story of Olara Otunnu told at the beginning of this booklet. At the very heart of some of the worst examples of abuse of power in the world today, a man is going about listening to ordinary people and telling their stories to the power-brokers. And as he builds these connections between the weak and the strong he is testifying to a connection between people that is deeper than the power differences that separate them. It is a risky strategy for all concerned. By refusing to give in to hatred, the Albanian hosts of Kosova's refugees and the African women working across tribal boundaries risk at best incredulity and at worst violent opposition. By listening to these stories and taking them seriously the ministers and generals risk having to surrender power, lose face and give up status in order to affirm goodness at the grass roots.

Otunnu's job of listening to the powerless and challenging the powerful requires both the capacity to hope and the ability to share despair. It requires the will to speak up and fight and the willingness to let go and accept defeat. But he is not alone. We have seen this capacity in present day public figures like Nelson Mandela and Mo Mowlam. We have seen it among our circle of friends and acquaintances and perhaps glimpsed it in ourselves. And, of course, we have seen it in Jesus.

To Do or Not To Do: Bible Study

Read the following two passages:

1 Samuel 16.1-4a, 6, 7, 10–12

The LORD said to Samuel, 'How long will you mourn for Saul, since I have rejected him as king over Israel? Fill your horn with oil and be on your way; I am sending you to Jesse of Bethlehem. I have chosen one of his sons to be king.' But Samuel said, 'How can I go? Saul will hear about it and kill

---

5 See Walter Wink, *The Powers That Be* (New York: Doubleday, 1998).

me.' The LORD said, 'Take a heifer with you and say, "I have come to sacrifice to the LORD." Invite Jesse to the sacrifice and I will show you what to do. You are to anoint for me the one I indicate.' Samuel did what the LORD said. When [Jesse and his sons] arrived, Samuel saw Eliab and thought, 'Surely the LORD's anointed stands here before the LORD.' But the LORD said to Samuel, 'Do not consider his appearance or his height, for I have rejected him. The LORD does not look at the things man looks at. Man looks on the outward appearance, but the LORD looks at the heart.' Jesse made seven of his sons pass before Samuel, but Samuel said to him, 'The LORD has not chosen these.' So he asked Jesse, 'Are these all the sons you have?' 'There is still the youngest,' Jesse answered, 'but he is tending the sheep.' Samuel said, 'Send for him; we will not sit down until he arrives.' So he sent and had him brought in. He was ruddy, with a fine appearance and handsome features. Then the LORD said, 'Rise and anoint him; he is the one.'

2 Samuel 12.1–7a

The LORD sent Nathan to David. When he came to him, he said, 'There were two men in a certain town, one rich and the other poor. The rich man had a very large number of sheep and cattle, but the poor man had nothing except one little ewe lamb that he had bought. He raised it, and it grew up with him and his children. It shared his food, drank from his cup and even slept in his arms. It was like a daughter to him. Now a traveller came to the rich man, but the rich man refrained from taking one of his own sheep or cattle to prepare a meal for the traveller who had come to him. Instead, he took the ewe lamb that belonged to the poor man and prepared it for the one who had come to him.' David burned with anger against the man and said to Nathan, 'As surely as the LORD lives, the man who did this deserves to die! He must pay for that lamb four times over, because he did such a thing and had no pity.' Then Nathan said to David, 'You are the man!'

Commentary

In the first of these passages we see David anointed as the future king of Israel by the old prophet Samuel. The kingship of Saul has come to an end because Saul cannot control the greed that leads him to hoard the spoils of war, rather than destroy them as God had commanded. In 1 Samuel 16 David is an innocent shepherd boy, far removed from the scheming of the royal court and the compromises of the battlefield. He represents a new start for the monarchy, a young man with a good heart who has not yet learnt to rely on himself. As the youngest of his brothers no-one expects David to be picked out by Samuel. But God's choice, mediated through the prophet, confirms the priority of the weak and overlooked in God's plan—a plan which the Israelite kings are called to make a reality. Ironically, despite making it clear that God looks on the heart, the author of the passage cannot resist telling us that David is handsome, falling into the familiar trap of equating God's power with human success.

The story unfolds. David defeats Goliath, battles with Saul, becomes king, leads armies in war and ends up orchestrating the death of his courtier Uriah so that he can sleep with Bathsheba his wife. Enter another prophet, this time Nathan, who confronts David with his fall from grace, likening him to an abusive and careless overlord who has no respect for those less powerful than himself. Kingly pretensions are exposed, the legitimacy of power is seen to pivot on its ability to deliver justice and David is thrown back on God's mercy.

Questions
- What are the risks associated with human power?
- What qualities does God look for in those who wield power?
- What is the role of the prophet?

4
Power and God

Then someone came to him and said, 'Teacher, what good deed must I do to have eternal life? And he said to him, 'Why do you ask me about what is good? There is only one who is good. If you wish to enter into life, keep the commandments.' He said to him, 'Which ones?' And Jesus said, 'You shall not murder; You shall not commit adultery; You shall not steal; You shall not bear false witness; Honour your father and mother; also, You shall love your neighbour as yourself.' The young man said to him, 'I have kept all these; what do I still lack?' Jesus said to him, 'If you wish to be perfect, go, sell your possessions, and give the money to the poor, and you will have treasure in heaven; then come, follow me.' When the young man heard this word, he went away grieving, for he had many possessions.

Matthew 19.16-22 (NRSV)

What is God's Power Like?
When Christians want to explore the divine we do not look directly at the mystery but at Jesus, God's revelation of himself on earth, who takes the creating and sustaining power of God in creation and models it in action in the world.

The gospels remind us that in his unique relationship with God, Jesus had divine power—the divine ability to *do* or to act—at his disposal. In the accounts of Matthew and Luke, Satan taunts Jesus in the desert with this fact of the difference in power between God and people, a difference that could give Jesus a chance to assert and protect himself: 'Then the devil led him up and showed him in an instant all the kingdoms of the world. And the devil said to him, "To you I will give their glory and all this authority; for it has been given over to me, and I give it to anyone I please. If you, then, will worship me, it will all be yours"' (Lk 4.5–7).

But Jesus rejects Satan's suggestion that he prove his divine potential with a show of strength. Instead, his power is used in the context of a quite breathtaking humility. After Peter's dramatic realization that Jesus is 'the Christ, the Son of the living God' in Matthew 16, Jesus forbids his disciples to acclaim his power, warning them not to tell anyone that he is the Christ (Mt 16.20). Throughout the gospels we read that he shared his ministry with ordinary men and women. He is accompanied everywhere by a band of fellow workers and friends (Lk 8.1–2) and commissions the twelve to cast out evil spirits in his name (Mk 6.7). To compound his rejection of the egotism, isolation and privilege that Satan offers, Jesus is to be found associating with those in the least powerful sections of society—the economically powerless like the disabled, widows and prostitutes, or those whose economic power masks a social vulnerability, like the despised tax collectors.

All these rejections of the temptation to abuse power are like steps leading to the ultimate relinquishment. Alone on the cross Jesus does not simply reap the bitter rewards of his denial of traditional, authoritative, self-protecting power. He becomes fundamentally identified with the powerless ones he has touched during his life, and with their choiceless experience of being 'done to.'

Yet far from being weak, this radical style of living and dying, and the shocking teaching that accompanies it, are powerfully compelling and life-changing both then and now. Though Jesus resisted being acclaimed an authority figure, crowds of people were drawn to him because his words had a compelling ring of truth. Though he relinquished power and status, his life on the streets caused thousands to live changed lives both then and now.

So What is This Powerless Power That Jesus Shows Us?

The gospels picture a power holder whose power is not coercive or abusive. He does not use his divine strength to guarantee his own future or to force followers. Rather his powerful teaching and actions in healing, naming and listening are directed outwards, empowering people to respond as they choose. Take the 'rich young ruler,' whose familiar story is told at the beginning of this chapter. He approaches Jesus of his own volition, perhaps drawn by rumours that Jesus has answers and driven by his own concern to be right with God. Jesus surprises him by answering his question about pleasing God with the traditional answer—obey the commandments. In fact the young man has to ask two supplementary questions before Jesus gives him the challenging response he was half hoping for and half dreading—sell your possessions, give to the poor and follow me. Rather than leaping straight into a lecture on the virtue of charity, Jesus' reticence gives space for the young man to get over his initial awkwardness in the presence of the great teacher and articulate his own burning question. Having really heard where the man is coming from, Jesus tells him straight, not hiding the challenge to relinquishment or wrapping it up to make it seem more palatable. But having done so, the young man is again given space for his own voice—there is no attempt to make him sign on the dotted line of commitment. He is allowed to walk away with the truth ringing in his ears.

Some say 'yes' to Jesus and some say 'no.' Some understand him, some do not. Some are hungry for his challenge and others resist it. Some want to touch him, others want to kill him. Jesus does not control their reactions—and he does not seem to mind.

Our definitions of God's power and of the power human beings are called to exercise are profoundly qualified by what we know about Jesus. His power was located in identification with—and assumption of—powerlessness. His authority was found not in his power over others but in his relationships with them. Rather than patronizing the powerless Jesus responded to them as one human being to another, sharing a meal, visiting a home, reaching out to touch. And this emphasis on relationships is as clear in the way he taught as in the way he interacted with people.

We know that Jesus commonly used parables—stories whose everyday surface hid a deeper meaning which kept his listeners guessing. Rarely did he impose an interpretation on a parable, treating his audience as partners in a dialogue rather than passive recipients of instruction. The parables provoke questioning, grumbling and engagement. There *is* authority in the words of Jesus, *and* submission to them by his followers, but the possibility of not submitting is always allowed.

Power and Trust

In this method of teaching and his training, Jesus showed that a childlike trust in God is the beginning and not the end. Rather than clinging to the safety of his presence, Jesus' followers are sent out to run the race for themselves as adults in a two way relationship with God. Jesus uses his power to confer personhood and dignity on ordinary people who would have been looked down on by the religious leaders as ignorant working men and women. He sees people's need not as a stage on which to play out his power, but as a backdrop to their own developing relationship with God. In Roland Riem's Grove booklet, *Power and Vulnerability: Reflections on Mark 9,* the author says those who pray like Jesus 'have the power to confer personhood on those whom society fears and calls victim.'[6] This is the empowering power of God—the power of grace that changes people freely.

Once again we are brought up sharp against the contrast between Jesus and our own ideas of what someone *like* Jesus should be like. If God is more powerful than us does that not mean he is in control of us, imposing his will on us whether we like it or not? Yet in Jesus we see that divine power does not impose or control. Instead it frees and empowers, 'reveal(ing) the authority of God to be in no way oppressive, inhibiting, external, alienating…but rather liberating, enabling, personal, sustaining and creative.'[7]

Power—the ability to do things—exists in God and comes from God into the world. But in Jesus it is not channelled through the division of things into us and them, God and people, weak and strong, but through relationships between those groups which break down barriers and check abuse. Jesus, the sign of God's power in the world, is found not only *with* the weak but as *one of* the weak. He reveals God to be not just an all-powerful transcendent being dispensing commands from on high, but an immanent person with whom we can have a relationship. This is not to undermine or deny the majesty of God's power in creating the world and overcoming the forces of chaos. But God as divine warrior, continually battling the forces of evil, expresses himself in the vulnerability of making connections, first with Israel and then with the whole of humanity in Jesus. Revealing himself as a baby in Bethlehem God makes vulnerable relationships the framework for exercising his power. Indeed the possibility of relating is intrinsic to the powerful creative force that asserts life over death and being over non-being.

This does not abolish differences of strength between people. But it does challenge us not to use those differences as a excuse to exploit one another or to accept exploitation. When God comes to earth we discern that the difference between us, though real, is not constituted by the assertion of power by one thing over another. Jesus models the difference between God and man, power and powerlessness, being drawn together in friendship. His approach to power is based on neither the oppressive state nor the autonomous individual, but on community.

6   Roland Riem, Power and Vulnerability: Reflections on Mark 9 (Grove Spirituality Series No 52, Nottingham: Grove Books Ltd, 1994) p 20.
7   Paul Avis, Authority, Leadership and Conflict in the Church (London: Mowbray, 1992) p 125.

To Do or Not To Do: Rewriting the Liturgy

Look at the words of the *Gloria in Excelsis* from the Anglican church's liturgy—or pick a similar form of words from your own church tradition. (The *Gloria* is an ancient prayer of praise used within the Anglican communion service to focus the mind and heart of the congregation on the God they have come to worship or in response to sharing communion.)

Glory to God in the highest,
and peace to his people on earth.

Lord God, heavenly King,
almighty God and Father,
we worship you, we give you thanks,
we praise you for your glory.

Lord Jesus Christ, only son of the Father,
Lord God, Lamb of God,
you take away the sin of the world:
have mercy on us;
you are seated at the right hand of the Father:
receive our prayer.

For you alone are the Holy One,
you alone are the Lord,
you alone are the Most High,
Jesus Christ,
with the Holy Spirit,
in the glory of God the Father. Amen.

Compose an alternative *Gloria* using words and phrases to describe God that reflect his powerlessness, his vulnerability and his immanence. To get started, change all the words that refer to strength or success—Lord, almighty, highest and so on.

5
Power and Us

So what does the vulnerable power of God mean for us? And in what ways might it affect our spirituality?

The metaphor of communication is helpful in unpacking this idea of vulnerable power. Communication is about speaking *and* listening. The power modelled by Jesus, which we aspire to emulate, is about being able to speak but choosing to listen.

Speaking

Jesus credits people with voices to accept or reject him, and we are called by him to have a voice and to know its power. Having a voice does not mean that we always say right or sensible or intelligible things. But it does mean that we have a deep down sense of our own dignity before God and before other people, founded on our relationships with them.

With our own voice we can say 'yes' and we can say 'no.' Just as with the 'rich young ruler,' Jesus never forces us to follow him or to believe in him. Instead he allows us to respond to his call (or not to respond) freely, rather than out of the choiceless necessity of being weak.

Having a voice means that we have boundaries. If we are to be adult members of society, there is a limit to how much responsibility for our lives we hand over to others. So also there is also a limit to how much security and certainty we should seek from God. Jesus offered his followers neither security or certainty—instead he offered a relationship with the divine within which to sail the sea of insecurity and uncertainty which is the reality of life on Earth.

Having a voice means knowing that God has faith in us and that he is at home in our questions and struggles. Having a voice means not just relating to God as humble supplicants or passive receptacles for his perfect plan, but battling and struggling and arguing with him in a relationship of trust. And finding our voice is not just about an inner sense of empowerment. As we are empowered so our voice speaks up for itself and has an impact in the world—getting things done, pointing things out, warning, encouraging, creating, nurturing, teaching and leading in the service of love and justice.

For some, the speaking part of the bargain is very hard—particularly for those whose voices have been denied, who have been treated as failures, felt rejected by God or who simply do not feel worthy or clever enough to speak up. We can get used to seeing ourselves as victims, caught in a logic of sacrifice which tells us we must abandon ourselves, our honesty and our desires to a demanding God or to abusive relationships or oppressive structures. For us, finding our voice might involve recovering our sense of choice before God. This may lead us through anger and sadness and away from God or from church for a time. But as we receive God's gift of our unique, adult voice, free to say what it wants to say rather than mouth what it has been told, we will be drawn closer to him in the end.

Listening

There is no communication without both speaking and listening. The assertive, speaking part of relating to power is not complete without the corresponding listening and letting go.

However powerful we may be—whether as an individual or simply as part of a wealthy and privileged society—the power that we experience and our ability to 'do' things is bounded by our ultimate powerlessness. We are created beings for whom life is an unaccounted gift and who will sooner or later die. Whatever we may achieve or acquire, we are at root dependent for our life on the power of God, the action of the creator breathing life into creation. Human life on earth must in the end let go into this mysterious and prior power. Our speaking, acting and asserting ourselves—even our ability to do good and to protect love and justice—will eventually cease.

It is natural to be afraid of this ultimate powerlessness and hard to accept the loving arms of God behind it. But acknowledging it prevents powerful speaking slipping into dominance. In *Wisdom of Fools*, Mary Grey says we must 'Listen to the message to let go of the obsessive need to control and dominate. Be not afraid of vulnerability, of powerlessness, of the body's mortality, of impotence in the face of the raging storm.'[8] We practice this vulnerability by building into our lives spaces to be silent, times to drink in the creativity of others, to listen to new ideas, and to lament the vulnerability of love and justice rather than always jumping in to protect it.

This listening side of the bargain is very hard for some of us. Listening can expose us to challenge, to upset, to voices that disturb and shake us. We prefer the feeling of safety that comes from having something to say. This urge for structure is natural to human beings and is given vent in the speaking part of the power equation. But the call to listen reminds us that however much we may know about God, our ultimate security must be found in the risk of leaning on mystery—a mystery incarnated to be *with us* in the mess at least as much as *over us* making sense of it.

As speakers and listeners we embrace life, using our power for good, and accept death, resting not on our own power but on the life-giver. We will find it much easier to listen if we have truly learned to speak. Speaking

---

8   Mary Grey, Wisdom of Fools (Great Britain: SPCK, 1993) p 136.

allows us to name our fears and our questions and to have them held by the divine listener, rather than simply being eternal listeners to an oppressive divine speaker. And we will find it easier to speak if we have truly learned to listen. The theologian Walter Brueggemann described a journeying God who is continually pilgrimaging toward newness.[9] By letting go of what we already have we open up an empty space to receive God's new gift. To do this will require a humble dependence on God and a willingness to risk engagement with his life-affirming and vulnerable power modelled in Jesus—power to create and to destroy, to build up and to throw down—which is part of the mysterious gift of being human.

To Do or Not To Do: Creating Speaking and Listening Rituals

Create a 'speaking' ritual to celebrate the life and the power to do good that you have.

A ritual is a familiar form of actions that helps express something deeply true beyond words. As we grow into our rituals they become safe and sacred spaces into which we can come to meet God—like putting on an old, familiar coat. Rituals can be anything from the patterns we follow in church to the way we set the table at home. A 'speaking' ritual to celebrate life could simply involve moving from a kneeling to a standing position, or coming forward to the communion table in church, to receive a commissioning prayer. Or it could involve actions like the giving of a seedling, an opportunity to take up tools of peace (bandages, agricultural tools, paper and pen), or the writing out of hopes and dreams to pin on an altar.

To take this exercise a stage further, design a whole 'speaking' liturgy or service to contain your ritual. This could include: prayers to thank God for your life, health and wealth such as they are; readings from the Bible and other sources about God's gift of life, the call to live life to the full, and the challenge to use the power we have to do good; sounds of life—a new born baby crying, a stream flowing, an inspirational speech; opportunities to give voice to the voiceless through testimony, through commissioned poems or prayer, or through egalitarian seating arrangements and distribution of roles.

Then create a 'listening' ritual to accept powerlessness and to prepare for the relinquishment and letting go of death. As before, this ritual could be a simple action like sitting with open hands or laying keys or some other symbol of power on the communion table. Or it could involve actions like touching the cross; placing blank pages on the table or receiving a symbolic blessing prayer or gift from one another. Again, this exercise can be developed by designing a 'listening' liturgy or service to house your ritual.

---

9 See Walter Brueggemann, Power, Providence and Personality (USA: Westminster/John Knox Press, 1990).

6
Power and the Church

To Do or Not To Do
1. Reorder Your Church

Take five minutes to sketch out a rough plan of your church building on a piece of scrap paper. Note the position of the pews, the entrances and exits, any special bits of furniture (like a table or font). Take a moment to picture the space full of people on Sunday morning. Note down where all the different people sit and stand during the service—the children, those who make the tea and coffee, the leader, the preacher, the person doing the prayers. Where do you sit? Bring to mind what all the different people are wearing. Does anyone wear a uniform or carry a special object at any point during the service? Finally, note any special actions that take place—bowing or genuflecting, raising hands in praise, facing east, taking a collection.

Take a look at your drawing and notes. What does the way that your community organizes itself on a Sunday show you about what it believes, perhaps unconsciously, about power?

Now let your imagination run wild on the second sheet of paper by redrawing the same space but this time consciously setting out to reorganize it so that it reflects an alternative attitude to power—listening as well as speaking, empowering as well as controlling. Apply this to the seating arrangements, the uniforms and the different roles and actions you identified earlier.

If you are really brave, show your plans to the vicar.

2. Practice Parables

Think of something you would really like to get done or something you have strong feelings about. It might be a project at work, a lesson you wish your children would learn or a strong political opinion. Imagine you have been given a chance to explain your idea to a captive audience.

Instead of planning out a three point speech to make your point, write a story—or parable—to express it. This is harder than it sounds and writing down your three points is still a useful way to get clear in your own mind what you want to say. When Jesus told parables he always peopled them with recognizable characters and used examples and situations from everyday life. And he let his stories speak for themselves, dropping them like seeds onto the fertile ground of his listeners' imaginations and allowing them to work out the meaning for themselves.

Once your story is written, tell it to someone, resisting the temptation to explain at the end. If you preach, try this exercise for your next sermon.

The Challenge of Power

'What is really required is a new understanding of authority which does not have power at its heart, whether authoritarian or libertine: an authority which has community and communion as its goal.'[10]

Jesus' demonstration of power mediated through relationships—and its development in the twin poles of speaking and listening—has implications for our church life, with challenges for both powerful and powerless.

We have seen that power slips into abuse when its protective and life-giving properties are used to bolster the strong. But remembering that power must be channelled and qualified in relationships keeps the seed of vulnerability alive and builds a barrier to corruption and misuse.

For the powerful, building this vulnerability into the way we lead means understanding that God is not just to be found in our mission statement, our prayer book, our way of doing things, our congregational market share. He is also present in people and things beyond the safe structures that legitimize our position. For the powerless, this affirmation of the presence of God outside power structures challenges us to reread our weakness as a sign of God and a potential place of revelation.

It is important to stress that this emphasis on God outside church structures is not to deny his presence within them. Rather it is to redress the imbalance between speaking and listening that humans so quickly fall into in the search for truth. The refusal to listen to the presence of God in the weak was something the Old Testament prophets identified when they looked at Israel's monarchy. They reminded the kings that God was speaking in the real experience and suffering of their people. Jesus demonstrated the ultimate kingly response to this reminder by removing himself from the status and power he could have enjoyed as a rabbi and risking his teaching in a life lived amongst his hearers. And in Jesus God casts off his divine power and makes his home within creation.

As a church, we need to ask ourselves how much this powerful relinquishment is reflected in our exercise of power today. How much do church structures indicate that God is present among ordinary people? And how much does teaching and preaching enable congregations to realize their status as adults in relationship with God? Robert Runcie has argued that the goal of Christian authority is 'the communion of free men and women with God and with each other.' How far do our churches allow this liberating communion and how far do they restrict it?

It is important for the church to at least be attempting to live out a different way of dealing with power, since its mission is to preach and to live the

---

10 Robert Runcie, Authority in Crisis: An Anglican Response (London: SCM Press Ltd, 1988) p 29.

'good news to the poor' modelled by Jesus (Lk 4.18). And this revolutionary gospel is not designed to keep things as they are but to create the new heaven and the new earth prophesied by Isaiah (11.6) and pictured in Revelation (21.22, 24), in which human power differences become meaningless in a new age of justice and equality.

Yet this commitment to living differently is not as common across the church as it should be. For example, a well known writer on church growth has said this: 'Working class people for the most part do not care to be part of the decision-making process. They feel uncomfortable if they are expected to come up with ideas.'[11] Not only is this highly offensive, it simply rewrites the injustice of the world as it is, seeing differences between people as an excuse for the dominance of the powerful. By denying the value of the 'weak,' it interprets their inability to speak in the dominant language as a justification for exclusion.

There is no protection against this sort of abuse without an understanding that people are connected to each other, and that the exercise of power is mediated through, and checked by, relationship.

To really take the world-changing mission of Jesus seriously we must affirm our connectedness to one another as God affirmed his connectedness to us in the incarnation. This means valuing all human experience as a potential locus of revelation. And it means, like God in Jesus, making the effort to go to the margins and speak the language of the people.

Questioning the Status Quo

This will lead us to some serious questions about our church practice. Is the church as democratic as it should be? How can we break down expectations that a priest or leader will be near-infallible? Why do we still 'enthrone' our bishops as if they were earthly kings and queens? Should it only be ordained clergy who can bless, absolve and preside at communion? These become more pressing as lay ministry and leadership in the church continues to increase. Indeed, lay involvement is perhaps the single biggest source of challenge to the power-hoarding tendency of the church institution.

To embrace connection across traditional power divides such as that between clergy and laity is a risky strategy. It is safer for the church to hold on to its power and avoid the risk of failure, incompleteness and imperfection that comes when we empower the community of faith. Choosing to take this risk demands a great depth of personal security rooted in God from those driving change. And it is only a first step, leaving many unanswered questions—not least how churches should respond when acknowledgement of

---

11 Peter C Wagner, Leading Your Church to Growth (United Kingdom: Hodder and Stoughton, 1978) p 93.

people's God-bearing potential means we find ourselves listening to voices that are unacceptably racist, sexist or anathema to the gospel. However, the point of exploring power dynamics in ourselves and God is exactly this—so that we can engage with the messy reality of the world, speaking and listening, getting it right and getting it wrong.

As Christians, we need not be afraid of power. It is part of God, part of us and part of the world we live in. Accepting our own ultimate powerlessness within God frees us to embrace the power within us to create and to change things without needing to cling on to that power for our own security. Every day the UN's Special Representative for Children, Olara Otunnu, sees the misuse and abuse of power met by the determination of ordinary people to fight for justice. Our faith is not just about acceptance and relinquishment. Rather these lay the foundations on which the power to change the world is built.